ART OF THE MENDE

University of Maryland Art Gallery
Department of Art

ART OF THE MENDE
UNIVERSITY OF MARYLAND ART GALLERY

Lenders to the Exhibition

THE AMERICAN MUSEUM OF NATURAL HISTORY, NEW YORK
JOSEPH J. BARGHAHN, WASHINGTON, D.C.
BALTIMORE MUSEUM OF ART
DR. AND MRS. BERNARD BERK, LUTHERVILLE, MD.
THE BROOKLYN MUSEUM
MARTIN FREDMANN, BALTIMORE
MICHAEL HEIDE, SEATTLE
MRS. SONJA HOLSEY, WASHINGTON, D.C.
BARBARA J. JACOBY, LOS ANGELES
MRS. JUDITH KAHAN, NEW YORK
MUSEUM OF AFRICAN ART, WASHINGTON, D.C.
THE MUSEUM OF PRIMITIVE ART, NEW YORK
NEW ORLEANS MUSEUM OFART
ROBERT AND NANCY NOOTER, WASHINGTON, D.C.
MRS.AND MRS. HAROLD ROME, NEW YORK
DR. JOSEPH SEIPP, BALTIMORE
MR. AND MRS. JAMES M. SILBERMAN, ARLINGTON, VA.
UCLA MUSEUM OF CULTURAL HISTORY
UNIVERSITY OF MARYLAND ART GALLERY, COLLEGE PARK
UNIVERSITY MUSEUM, UNIVERSITY OF PENNSYLVANIA, PHILADELPHIA

© 1974 The University of Maryland
Library of Congress Catalogue Card No. 74-77367
Printed and bound by Intelligencer Printing Company, Lancaster, Pa.
Designed by Richard Klank
Photographs courtesy of Duane Suter; Charles Uht; Susan Einstein; Paul Draper;
Stuart Lynn; Delmar Lipp; Robert Nooter; The Brooklyn Museum; and the
University Museum, University of Pennsylvania.

Cover: Bundu Dancer, Kpetema,
          Begbe Chiefdom, Bo District

ART OF THE MENDE

Catalogue by William L. Hommel
Organized under a grant from the Interpretive Exhibition Program,
  National Endowment for the Humanities

Art Gallery
University of Maryland, Department of Art
College Park
March 18–April 19, 1974

Museum of Art
University of Iowa
Iowa City
May 1–June 5, 1974

Newport Harbor Art Museum
Newport Beach, California
June 18–July 20, 1974

University Art Museum
University of Texas
Austin
September 1–October 13, 1974

NJAYEI ceremony, Taninahum
Bumpe Chiefdom, Bo District

The Mende exhibition is the very first exhibition devoted to African art ever organized by the Gallery of the Art Department of the University of Maryland. The initiation of such a show should not be misconstrued as a mere attempt to be "relevant." Our Mende exhibition does, of course, reflect the increasing interest in all aspects of black culture which is presently exemplified on so many levels of our national awareness. We are happy to acknowledge this fact. However, the meaning of this exhibition definitely transcends this notion. Above all, in our Department, we are concerned with art and the Mende art offers to us, to the University, and to the public at large, a most beautiful and a most exciting instance of aesthetic imagination and creativity. We believe that this kind of experience is not really so different from the experience which can be derived from an exhibition of French, Chinese, or American art. Art is one.

The organization of the exhibition is due to the combined and fruitful efforts of Dr. Eleanor Green and Mr. William Hommel. I should like to take this opportunity to express my admiration and appreciation for their industry and scholarship. Many other members of our Department should be thanked in this context. In particular I should like to thank Mrs. Jean Federico, secretary and acting registrar, Mr. Joseph Shannon, who did so much to achieve the success of the physical arrangement of the exhibition in the Gallery, and Professor Richard Klank who designed the catalogue. We should also acknowledge the assistance of several students, particularly Linda Simon and Edward Schiesser.

An exhibition of this scope could not be achieved without the help of other academic units of the University. I am very happy to congratulate Joe O'Connor who is responsible for the film which accompanies the exhibition and Professor Gene Weiss who acted as a friendly consultant in the field of film making. We have also had the support and consideration of the government of Sierra Leone and are most grateful for their assistance.

Of course we are deeply grateful to the National Endowment for the Humanities for the opportunity to undertake an exhibition of such magnitude and to the administration of the University, which has always displayed such a positive response to our needs.

George Levitine   *Chairman* Department of Art

On behalf of the Art Gallery of the University of Maryland, I would like to thank the staff of the Interpretive Exhibition Program of the National Endowment for the Humanities for their fine cooperation in all phases of the organization of this exhibition. In addition to funding the project, they have been continually helpful—from initial discussion of the grant application to final questions on technical problems of audio-visual presentations.

On the suggestion of the National Endowment for the Humanities, we sought a professional film maker at the last minute to accompany our principal investigator, William Hommel to Sierra Leone in the summer of 1973. On the recommendation of Dr. Thomas Aylward and Dr. Gene Weiss, the documentary film maker, Joe O'Connor, was asked to quickly change his summer plans, apply for a visa and leave within weeks to film in Africa. He has spent a good deal of the fall and winter editing and printing the four loops of ceremonial dances and the feature film that expands this exhibition. His dedication to the project is very much appreciated.

I should also like to thank the directors of other museums participating in the exhibition for their support: Ulfert Wilke, University of Iowa; James Byrnes, Newport Harbor Art Museum; and Donald Goodall, University of Texas at Austin.

The resources of the Art Gallery have been considerably strained by the scope of this exhibition; however, our small staff of faculty and graduate assistants has extended itself magnificently to solve the myriad problems. Jean Federico has edited and typed the catalogue and helped in organizing the exhibition; Roberta Diemer has copied and printed many of the field photographs; Sharman McGurn has organized group tours and handled publicity for the exhibition; Richard Klank and his graduate assistant Linda Simon have seen the catalogue through production; and Joseph Shannon and Edward Schiesser have designed and installed the exhibition. As always, George Levitine, Chairman of the Department of Art, has been generous in his support of the Gallery activities.

Finally, because it is most important, it should be noted that the entire exhibition from conception to installation is the brainchild of William Hommel, Associate Director of the Art Gallery. He is to be congratulated as well as thanked.

Eleanor Green
Director
Art Gallery

First I would like to thank the National Endowment for the Humanities for the grant which helped finance this exhibition. The generous assistance of the Sierra Leone Ministries of the Interior and Information and Broadcasting as well as the National Museum and Fourah Bay College greatly facilitated the research. Pastor Tom Stevens and J. J. Kebbie arranged for us to observe several ceremonies in which the sculpture is used. Amadu Kamara and Moisi of Nganyahun carved masks and figures in the traditional style to be included in the exhibition.

Leland Dresser, Reggie Hodges, and the Peace Corps provided hospitality and valuable information.

The catalogue has been greatly aided by the editorial comments of Roy Sieber and Eleanor Green. The staff of the Art Gallery has spent many extra hours in preparing this exhibition.

A special thanks to my wife, Barbara, and my children for their assistance and patience during the research and preparation of the exhibition.

William L. Hommel
Associate Director
Art Gallery

Introduction

Movement, music, light—the presence of the group and the spirit evoked—are all part of the Mende aesthetic expression. To be most enjoyed, the sculpture must be seen in motion; to be understood, it must be considered within the context of its ritual purpose. The mask without costume, or the figure isolated on a pedestal, reveals only a fraction of its essence. No exhibition in America can recreate the aesthetic experience of Mende ceremonies. It is hoped, however, that music and film will simulate some of the ambiance of the ritual.

Africa has, until recently, been so little understood that its art has been lumped together as if it all sprang from the needs and aesthetics of a single cultural group. Now, as the individual cultures are studied, the diversity of styles becomes apparent, and it is readily seen that the artistic sensibility of the Mende, from Sierra Leone, for example, is very different from that of the Dogon, the Dan, or the Yoruba. Studying a number of sculptures from a single cultural unit allows for examination of stylistic subtleties of production within that unit and permits placing the objects in their cultural/ritual context.

Most Mende art is created to be used in religious ceremonies. Masks, which embody spiritual forces, can perform outside their religious context, when called upon to help the village celebrate a festive occasion. The object's embodiment of a spirit during the ritual is demonstrated by certain restrictions such as the costume which totally covers the Bundu dancer protecting her from the spirit. Its spiritual orientation is further emphasized by the object being designed to appeal aesthetically to the spirits. Once the object has received this spiritual acceptance, as evidenced by continued use, it can no longer be analyzed critically. Many of the forms incorporated in the objects are symbols of concepts which the community wishes to convey to the spirits.

In Mende religion Ngewo, creator and ruler of the universe, is assisted by the ancestors and other Nga-fa (spirits) who act as intermediaries with man. Nga-fa refers to all spiritual manifestations including the personal soul and the masked participants of the socio-religious organizations. Ngewo and the Nga-fa are only important for the services such as protection and fertility, which they can render to the individual or the community.

Some works of Mende art are designed to enhance the prestige of the person who commissions them, such as the political hierarchy of chiefs and paramount chiefs.

Occasionally utilitarian objects such as the heddle pulley, part of a loom, or bars used to support a hammock are decorated with carved heads or other graceful designs. These decorated objects were not restricted to the ownership by chiefs, but their cost put them out of the reach of most people.

BUNDU Dancers, Kenema

Bundu Masks

The Bundu helmet mask, which embodies the guardian spirit of the exclusively female Sande society, is the only African mask reserved for use by women. The mask, also referred to as Sowei, is ubiquitous among the different cultures of Sierra Leone and Western Liberia. This tradition was probably spread by the Mende as they expanded throughout the area, although it may have originated with the Sherbro before their arrival. Some say the mask was first presented to the Sande society by the water spirit, Mamy Wata, others talk of a sympathetic carver who presented the leaders of the society with a facial cover so they could appear in public. It can only be said with certainty on the basis of early photographs and descriptions[1], that the style has been continuous for at least a century.

When a woman reaches the middle level of the Sande society, she commissions a mask which will be hers alone, and will project the personality of a particular spirit. She is the only person who evokes the spirit with the mask, so when she retires or moves upward in the society it becomes valueless and is either retired, transformed to represent the comedian, Gonde, or presented to a chief as a prestige gift. It is extremely important that a new mask be attractive to the spirit, otherwise it will not choose to enter, and the helmet is worthless. On attaining the middle level of the Sande society a woman seeks out a carver who, because of his profession, has more familiarity with the rituals and symbolism of the society than other men. She need tell him only the name it will bear before he secludes himself in the bush to visualize the personality of the spirit which will eventually inhabit it. The variations on the prototype expressing perhaps "motherly authority" or "scrutiny" are subtle and often lost when the mask is seen outside of ceremonial context. They are, however, kept in mind by the artist from the moment he cuts a log to the size of the mask with his machete.

To hold the log firm while it is transformed into a mask, Moisi, the sculptor observed at work, dug a hole in the ground and placed one end of the log in it. He then began digging out the head cavity with a long handled chisel and used a curved blade to scoop out the interior wood. This sculptor worked directly, in the traditional manner, without preliminary sketching.[2] After removing the hollowed log from the hole, Moisi marked what would become the center of the face along the length of the wood with his machete. From this center line he first roughed out a diamond shape and then proceeded to carve the face, hairstyle, and neck. Throughout the creative process he referred constantly to the original center line and to a horizontal line that intersected at the center of the face so that all the elements would be balanced and symmetrical in relation to the center point. If it is in keeping with the personality of the mask, the artist may tilt the head slightly on the neck; nevertheless, his concern for rhythmic repetition is retained as the eye slits are made carefully parallel to the mouth. The artist may choose to make the viewing slits correspond to the mask eyes or conceal them in the neck ridges. There are also constants in the forms prescribed by the iconography, although there will be variations from one region to another.

The symbolism, often physical and sexual as well as spiritual, is based on specific traditional concepts. The three lobed hair arrangement of the Kpa-Mende masks symbolizes maleness and acts as the physical complement in the women's society. Three and the corresponding female number, four, are found among many of the Mande speaking people.[3] Phallic symbolism is also associated with the projections above the center lobe and with the projections from the top of masks without lobes. This projection is a modification of the more literally depicted phallic symbol set in the center of a specially prepared meal served just before the young women are released from the Sande bush school to become brides. Another Kpa-Mende variation has a five lobed hair style symbolizing the vagina with the clitoris represented by the same forms as the phallus.[4]

The Sherbro-Mende carve a seven lobed hair style on their masks to present the concept of the complete human unit. Seven generally replaces the three and four even in the performance of the funerary ritual among the Sherbro-Mende.

The pyramidal form on the top of some masks represents the Sande shrine house. The bird is said to lighten the weight of the mask. The fish refers to river spirits such as Mamy Wata. The serpent found on some masks as well as sculptures of Mamy Wata may symbolize the spirit and the river, or it may be the boa constrictor considered responsible for sickness and death. Three

1. BUNDU MASK WITH RAFFIA, 15
    Carved 1896, Sembehun, Moyamba District
    Collection of Dr. Joseph Seipp, Baltimore

2. BUNDU MASK, 18¾
    Carved 1906, Mano Chiefdom, Moyamba District
    Collection of Dr. Joseph Seipp, Baltimore

4. BUNDU MASK, 15
    Carved 1918, Mano Chiefdom, Moyamba District
    Collection of Martin Fredmann, Baltimore

12. BUNDU MASK, 15
    Boyadu, Kenema District
    Lent Anonymously

8. BUNDU MASK, 15½
Collection of the New Orleans Museum of
Art
Gift of Mr. and Mrs. Walter Davis, Jr.

13. BUNDU MASK, 16
Kowama, Moyamba District
Lent Anonymously

10. BUNDU MASK, 13¾
Vai-Mende
Collection of The Museum of Primitive
Art, New York

6. BUNDU MASK, 16½
Vai-Mende
Collection of the UCLA Museum of Cul-
tural History, Gift of the Wellcome Trust

vertical incised lines under each eye of the mask correspond to scarification markings given in the bush school, while the markings extending from the corners of the eyes represent the medicine marks a mother gives her child shortly after birth for protection. Another form of protection, animal horns filled with fetish material, is represented in hair decorations.

Iconography from outside sources also appears. The cross or X was adapted from the markings of the Fanti when they began to intermarry with the Mende[5]. The X's inscribed on squares intertwined in the hair, however, represent quotes from the Koran or other Islamic writings. These texts are encased in pouches by the Mori men and worn, because they incorporate the spiritual power of Islam. Their use in the mask symbolism is indicative of the importance with which this power is viewed.

The bulging neck is both symbolic and functional. It is an expression of the Mende equation of corpulence to fertility and an exaggeration of the well fed appearance nubile women have on release from the Sande bush school. By enlarging the neck the artist is able to include it in the helmet form. The swelling of the gently rounded forms is reinforced by the attention given by the sculptor to smoothness of surface. In the final stages of making a mask, Moisi, for example, takes great care while working with a small knife to achieve continuous flowing planes and has recently begun using sandpaper to produce a satiny finish.

When the carving and sanding are completed, holes are burned in the bottom of the helmet where raffia will be attached, and it is dyed with the juice of leaves from the Kojo vine. When first applied, the juice turns the wood bright green, but it soon oxidizes to the desired deep brown.

As a final test before submitting the mask to his client, the sculptor performs a ceremony to determine in his own mind if it is satisfactory for spiritual use. If it passes this test, the woman who commissioned it will compare it with masks that have in the past proved pleasing to the spirit and, if she decided it is satisfactory, will accept it and perform a ritual which invites the spirit to enter. Before the spirit can enter, however, the costume must be completed to cover the entire body. Black-dyed raffia is attached to the mask, a cloth suit with the ends of the sleeves sewn closed, is worn over long stockings; the dancer often wears shoes

as a precaution against holes in the stockings. Any exposure of the body would allow the spirit to enter the dancer rather than the mask.

It may require several rituals before the spirit chooses to inhabit the mask; once this occurs the mask is no longer a simple object subject to aesthetic criticism. It embodies the power of the Bundu spirit and is only thought of in the totality of the rituals which govern a good deal of the lives of Mende women.

Girls first come under the control of the Bundu spirit upon entering the bush school at puberty, when they are trained in farming, cooking, child care, midwifery, Sande dances and songs, and use of herbal medicine—in short, all the skills they will need in the adult community. Here the spirit is a guardian and figure of authority. She escorts the girls from the village to the bush, supervises their training, anesthetizes by hypnosis during ritual surgery, and presides over their dismissal as she and senior members of the Sande society, sit and receive the wedding gifts presented the girls by prospective bridegrooms.

Different occasions for appearance of the Bundu spirit require different decorum. At solemn functions, such as the dismissal of the young women, she is reserved, leading the women into the village and then seating herself during the ceremony.[6] When the Bundu spirit entertains at public celebrations, however, she dances animatedly with much twirling, bowing, and forward and side movements. The choreography is lively and graceful, but always in keeping with the personality originally conceived in the mask and reflected in its carving. Some burst with energy, tipping head and shoulders in continuous counterpuntal movements with the rhythm of the music; others interrupt the rhythm with a stop-action scrutiny of the spectators; still others restrain themselves to movements appropriate to their matronly appearance.

It is in the dance context that the Bundu mask is seen to full effect as the light reflects from the facets giving the sculpture a constantly changing image. Unlike most European sculpture, meant to be perceived as the viewer circumnavigates the piece, these masks reveal themselves to the stationary spectator through the movement of the dancer. Mende art is almost exclusively sculptural, visualized from its conception as three dimensional flowing forms with textures which invite handling and turning.

The smoothness of the face is played off against the ridged hairstyle. The realistic softness of the face and neck is contrasted with the incised hairstyles and more abstract rendering of symbolic forms. The dance movements which are probably more emphatic in private ceremonies hint at the importance of the symbolism. But, even to the outsider, it is clear that the mask is a presence in itself. It is not merely a decorative object used to conceal or transform the personality of the wearer. Clothed as a woman in a cloth head wrapper, it is a presence in itself—a being.

This being, or personage, may also sit in judgment without the accompaniment of music. If a man violates the Sande law he will be brought before the Bundu spirit. Sitting silently she will assess the fine by communicating through the Digbas, the lowest member of the Sande society.

Silence is the eloquence of the Bundu spirit. The presence of the mask speaks for itself, but when it is no longer suitable as a receptical for the spirit, or if initially it did not measure up to the aesthetic standards for the Bundu, it may become the guise of the talking comedian, Gonde. When this happens the mask is often painted red and white in a kind of anti-aesthetic parody of the original. Bundu is silent and aloof; Gonde is light-hearted. She intermingles with the spectators, engaging them in dance or conversation. The contrast from the behavior expected of the sober Bundu extends even to frivolous wearing of borrowed hats and glasses. It is an ironic transformation. However, it is not always the fate of the one-time home of the Bundu spirit.

Some masks, after they complete their ritual existence, are decorated with silver or other metals and presented to the paramount chief. If the chief is female, she is often the active head of the Sande. If male, he is only the nominal head of all organizations in his district. In either case, the mask, often embellished with silver in a repoussé design, is presented to acknowledge the organization as part of the chief's domain. Beautiful as these masks may be, they no longer embody the spirit. With the addition of metal they become prestige rather than ritual objects.

23. GONDE MASK WITH COSTUME, 15
Collected at Bembe, Sitia Chiefdom
Sherbro Island, Bonthe District, 1936–37
Collection of the University Museum, University of Pennsylvania, Philadelphia

24. GONDE HELMET WITH SMALL HEAD, 14
Collection of Dr. and Mrs. Bernard Berk,
Lutherville, Md.

25. SANDE (GONDE HELMET?) FIGURE, 16
Collection of Barbara J. Jacoby, Los Angeles

Notes

[1] T. J. Alldridge, "Wanderings in the Hinterland of Sierra Leone," *The Geographical Journal* 4, no. 2 (August 1894) p. 136 and Alldridge, *The Sherbro and Its Hinterland,* New York, 1901, pp. 140–142.

[2] Some sculptors first sketch with charcoal on the wood, but this appears to be a recent innovation.

[3] These numbers establish the date for important events during and after life. For three days after marriage a woman sits idle on the veranda accepting the attention of the village. Rituals take place three days after death for women and four days for a man.

[4] Among other Mande speaking groups the clitoris is associated with maleness and its removal during ritual surgery leaves the women totally female. The Mende look upon the operation as helping the woman in childbirth, which may be an adaptation of the idea held by the other Mande speaking people or an example of the original purpose no longer being remembered by the people. It may also be one of the Sande secrets which are not to be revealed to outsiders.

[5] The Fanti of Ghana began fishing the rivers in Sierra Leone after fishing the coastal waters. The Mende agriculturalists felt no conflict with the Fanti fishermen.

[6] She will sometimes conceal herself behind a mat held by another member of the society in order to lift or tilt her mask for relief from the heat.

BUNDU Dancer, Kenema

Sande Musical Staff

The staffs, which have a ball encased in the open-work design, are used by the Bundu spirit and the senior members of the society as symbols of authority and as musical instruments. One end of the staff is always carved with a miniature of the Bundu mask. An example in the exhibition has this form at both ends.

The sculpture, which has a sphere at one end, is handled by the artist as if the staff was a string of spheres. Even the head described only by a hairstyle, is carved to correspond to the other end of the staff. The repetition of spheres interrupted by two open-work segments and a spool-like handle sets up a rhythmic pattern in the staff.

The staff with the Bundu head on each end reflects a rhythmic counterbalance by reversing the head and beveled neck motif separated by the open center design. The hairstyles on this piece are done in the seven lobes of the Sherbro-Mende area.

30. MUSICAL STAFF WITH TWO HEADS, 18¼
     Carved at Sembehu, Sitia Chiefdom, Sher-
     bro Island, Bonthe District
     Collected 1936–37
     Collection of the University Museum, Uni-
     versity of Pennsylvania, Philadelphia

31. MUSICAL STAFF WITH WOMAN'S COIFFURE,
     19
     Collected from Chief of Tome
     Sherbro Island, Bonthe District, 1936–37
     Collection of the University Museum,
     University of Pennsylvania, Philadelphia

Sande Medicine Figure

There is a sculpture similar in form to a Bundu mask, which is solid and usually only about five to ten inches high. These miniature heads, as well as full female figures with hands on their breasts, are used as protectors or part of the Sande medicine. The hands on the breasts emphasize femininity and symbolize the exclusive female membership of the organization. They are kept in a screened-off portion of the Sande shrine house, which is also occupied by the principal woman of the society. Their primary use is to cure an illness, caused by a person's transgression against the Sande. Illness is considered to be the result of some spiritual displeasure. The figure is used to bring spiritual aid in a person's recovery, while herbs are used to give physical aid.

This type of figure is also used in cases of injury. While I was observing Moisi carving the Bundu mask, my four year old son was playing nearby and fell on a rock which caused a large cut on his forehead. Moisi was very upset because he bled profusely. I told Moisi that we would return in a few days, and we took my son to a dispensary which was about fifteen miles away and had his cut sutured. When I returned, Moisi had carved a small Sande medicine head which he told me was for my son who had been hurt. About a week after my son received it, a small woodworm hole developed in the sculpture in the same position as the injury on his forehead. He developed no infection and has a very small scar, even though the sutures were not effective.

27. SANDE MEDICINE FIGURE, 23½
    Collection of the Museum of African Art,
    Washington, D.C.
    Gift of Robert and Nancy Nooter

29. SANDE MEDICINE HEAD, 11⅝
Collection of the UCLA Museum of Cultural History
Gift of the Wellcome Trust

26. SANDE MEDICINE HEAD, 9
Collected at Mokele, Kagboro Chiefdom
Sherbro Island, Bonthe District, 1936–37
Collection of the University Museum, University of Pennsylvania, Philadelphia

GOBOI, Mano-Njebla
Nongowa Chiefdom, Kenema District

FALUI, Bumpe, Bo District (right page)

Poro Masks

Goboi, Yavi, Jobai, Falui, and Nafoli are spirit-inhabited masks of the powerful men's Poro society which appear in public. Each plays a different part in the rituals of this socio-religious institution which is pervasive in Sierra Leone, Guinea, Liberia, and part of the Ivory Coast.

Of these, Goboi appears to be the most potent. He is important in funerary and initiation rites, remains to entertain the community after ceremonies, and appears at festivals.

His head of leather and brightly colored cloth is drum-shaped with panels of leather hanging from four places. His body of long loose raffia falls as a cone over the dancer's shirt and trousers of woven cotton. Raffia cuffs cover the hands and feet. Much of the front is covered by a large piece of hide.

On Goboi's back is an oval arrangement of small wooden plaques with a tail of animal skin below it. Each of the plaques is inscribed with quotes from the Koran written in Arabic. As with the symbols on the Bundu masks, the power of Islam is thus added to the power of the spirit.[1]

When young men have completed their training in the Poro bush school, they are welcomed back to the community as full adult members. This celebration is open only to members of the Poro so Goboi drives the women and children from the area before the appearance of the sacred spirit who wears a wooden mask but never appears in public.

Even when he entertains in public celebrations, Goboi retains an aspect of fear. As he enters, he rushes at the young boys often causing them to fall over each other as they try to avoid the sweep of his costume. Their fear is mitigated by the reassurance of the other spectators, but their faces retain an expression of awe as long as Goboi is present.

The arrival of Goboi is announced by three attendants, the Wujangas, who groom and control him during the dance. In a cycle repeated several times during the ceremony he mimes a wild animal who breaks into rages of frantic movement and then is subdued by the attendants using a twig whip. While docile, he stands restlessly as the Wujangas comb his raffia hair with twigs and fan him with a wicker tray.

Yavi, who also appears on ceremonial occasions with Gbenie, is less intimidating than Goboi. His body is more nearly human with legs and arms formed in the costume. The head is covered

in colored cloth and round mirrors with yarn-wrapped upright projections at the corners. Like Goboi, he is impersonated by a minor Poro official in a dance that alternates between states of agitation and calm.

Jobai, who resembles Yavi and Goboi, in a garb of conical raffia topped by a cubical headpiece of leather or wood inlaid with mirrors, is controlled by the younger members of the Poro. In fact, boys who have not yet completed their training in Poro often construct their own version out of palm branches topped by a small cluster of flowers and entertain while practicing the dance they will perform later in the larger costumes. Jobai also has attendants to calm and groom him and to guide him through the crowd as he twirls while rising and shrinking. To emphasize the spiritual aspect of Jobai, the dancer, at one point, shrivels until the raffia lies flat on the ground, the headpiece askew in the center with no evidence of human occupation.

Falui who appears in celebrations as an entertainer is also under the control of a young group within the Poro. He arouses no fear even though he speaks in a secret language of restructured Mende and has the authority to flog anyone, regardless of rank, for improper behavior. He appears in a long piece of woven country cloth attached around the ankles and fringed with raffia. On his head he wears a tall, red, conical cap topped with feathers. A flap of monkey fur, which can periodically be lifted to see where he is going, hangs over the face as he executes intricate side steps. He must never remove or lose the headdress or reveal his identity, however, or he will be fined for compromising the spiritual integrity of the mask.

Nafoli is another popular entertainer. He wears rice sacking sewn into a shirt, trousers, and a hood that completely covers his head. Aside from slits cut to permit vision, the hood is completely covered with paint and mirrors. He performs intricate dances and acrobatic stunts such as climbing a tall thin pole or bouncing high up in the air from a heavy net. They are the spirit of youth and often include young boys in their troupe.

[1]Small bottles containing the ink, which has been washed off tablets of Islamic writing, and prayers and quotes from the Koran written on paper and encased in leather are also carried to add the protection of Islam.

JOBAI, Taninahun
Bumpe Chiefdom, Bo District

Njayei Mask

The Njayei society's elongated, spotted mask embodies a spirit which controls the flow of life force. Illness among the Mende is considered to be a lessening of the life force in an individual who has caused the displeasure of a spirit or gone against the rules of a secret society.

The main concern of the Njayei is the regulation of sexual conduct. Intercourse in the bush is often punished by impotence. The impotent man consults a soothsayer to determine the cause of his problem and then is sent to the Njayei society to arrange for a ceremony at which the mask will appear. The spirit is called upon to aid in such diverse problems as mental illness, fertility, self confidence, and personality development.

The Njayei society membership consists of both men and women, but they must first be members of either Sande, Poro, or Wunde. The head of the society is a woman whose house is also the society shrine.

The mask is symbolic of the function of the spirit, especially the sexual and fertility aspects. The elongated form and the ridge on the top of the mask create a phallic representation. During the ceremony two women approach the mask and the spectators while performing an erotic dance. This dance ritual is a form of sympathetic magic—the interaction between the dancers and the mask conveys the concept of fertility to the spirit asking him to bring this blessing to the individuals or community.

The male symbolism of the mask is further indicated by the figure wearing a circular red cloth pouch which is decorated with three cowrie shells, the male number. The movement of the mask is restricted to swaying back and forth while in a bent over position which reveals and emphasizes the top of the mask. Its forward movement consists of only a few steps before the figure sits down on the stool again. The mask might be considered more an observer than a participant in the ceremony since it remains seated during most of the ritual. When the spirit has received the

NJAYEI Ceremony, Taninahun,
Bumpe Chiefdom, Bo District

message of the ritual, the masked figure returns to the shrine house.

The spotted markings on the mask are an important insignia of the Njayei society. They are found on the stool as well as the sword used by one of the women dancers during the ceremony. The round shrine house is similarly decorated with dark brown spots. These markings appear to be placed on the ceremonial objects just before the ritual by dotting them with red and white earth pigments. The red is symbolic of blood which is closely associated with life force and, therefore, with health and fertility. The white is associated with the spirits. The dark brown of the mask symbolizes fertility. These color symbols are found in garments of the mask's attendant who is dressed in white and wears a red head-ring decorated with white cowrie shells.

The simple lines of the mask with the ears and mouth indicated in low relief and only the nose projecting boldly below the protruding forehead emphasizes the importance of the whole rather than the representation of a face. The angularity of the eyes, forehead ridge, and bottom of the nose are contrasted with the rounded ears, mouth, and the gently curving nose and outline of the mask. The smooth curve of the top ridges is contrasted with angular incised lines of decoration.

34. NJAYEI MASK WITH RAFFIA, 21
Lent Anonymously

Clay Mortar

A gracefully carved mortar is used for the grinding of the white clay associated with the spiritual world and especially the ancestors. The mortar is usually a depressed surface supported by an open-work base with a long beveled neck and a head projecting from one end. According to Zeller[1] these were used by the Sande society to grind white clay which was then mixed with water to form a body coating.

The bodies of the girls are painted with this mixture for many rituals during their training. During their dismissal ceremony the Sande initiates enter the village with their bodies coated for the final time, before they go to the river for the ritual washing and dressing in their wedding garments.

These mortars are also used to grind the clay into the fine white powder which is mixed with herbs and medicines administered by the Bundu, Njayei, Yassi, and Humoi societies.

The delicately carved head at the end of the beveled neck contrasts with the more angular treatment of the body of the mortar. The rounded depression repeats the general outline of the head. The artist uses the long beveled neck, characteristic of Mende art, to combine symbol with function in the handle.

[1]Rudolf Zeller, "Die Bundu-Gesellshaft," *Jahresbericht des Historischen Museums in Bern,* 1912, pp. 114–115.

55. Clay Mortar, 12½
      Collection of the UCLA Museum of Cultural History, Gift of the Wellcome Trust

50. MEDICINE FIGURE. 12¾
Collection of Joseph J. Barghahn

Medicine Figures

Similar to the Sande, the Njayei, Humoi, and Yassi societies use figure sculpture as protectors and curative agents. Although the societies are separate and distinct, the style of the societies is so similar that it is often impossible, without knowing the provenance of a specific piece, to determine its origins. Typically, the sculptures are standing female figures with the arms carved free of the body, and sometimes, with the hands on the hips. Occasionally a Humoi figure is found with a bent neck indicating the punishment for a transgression of regulations. There is also an example of a Njayei figure in the Sierra Leone museum with arms raised and hands resting on the side of the head, but these variations are rare.

The structures of the societies as well as their sculptures are similar. All three are open to both men and women, and all are concerned with medicine and sexual behavior.

The Njayei and the Humoi, found among the same groups of Mende, even have reciprocal privileges for their members.

The Sherbro-Mende Yassi is a variation of the Kpa-Mende Njayei society. Both apply spotted decoration to their shrines and other ceremonial objects and have women dancing with swords during their rituals. The exceptions to the spotted decoration are the medicine figures which are stained a dark brown or black. They are kept in a special area of the shrine with the medicine and, when needed to perform a cure, are placed in a bowl with an herb and clay mixture, which produces the characteristic spotted design of the societies. Thus the physical and spiritual needs of the afflicted are served simultaneously.

The Yassi Minsereh figure illustrated was described in its original setting as, ". . . kept in a small compartment in the Yassi house and guarded by a wooden image representing a woman official of the Society. The figure stands in a bowl, which may be carved in one piece with it, in which the 'medicine' is placed when it is brought out for the treatment of a person who has been 'affected' by it."[1]

[1] H. U. Hall, *The Sherbro of Sierra Leone*, Philadelphia, 1938, p. 6.

41. MEDICINE FIGURE, 27¾
    Collection of Barbara J. Jacoby, Los Angeles
36. MEDICINE FIGURE, 29
    Collection of Mr. and Mrs. Harold Rome, New York
42. MEDICINE FIGURE, 20
    Collection of the Museum of African Art, Washington, D.C.
    Gift of Lawrence Gussman
46. YASSI MEDICINE FIGURE IN BOWL, WITH ALUMINUM, 17¾
    Collected at Kawno, Sitia Chiefdom, Sherbro Island, Bonthe District, 1936–37
    Collection of the University Museum, University of Pennsylvania, Philadelphia

Gongoli

Gongoli is comic. Asymmetrical, oversized, out of proportion, with mismatched features, he contradicts all the aesthetic norms of serious Mende art; he is funny because he is ridiculous.

These relationships are evident from an early point in the carving. The Gongoli mask carved for the exhibition by Amadu Kamara has large bulging cheeks and a forehead which overpowers the eyes and reduces them to slits. Once the basic contour of the mask was carved, Amadu took a piece of charcoal and marked the place for these forms with large circles. He also emphasized the mouth with protruding teeth. While carving, he concentrated on these forms and worked the rest of the sculpture around them. At certain times during the carving, Amadu would hold the mask in front of his face while going through some of the movements of the Gongoli dancer; then he would begin to laugh as he visualized the audience's reaction.

A padlock or cow's horn may dangle from one ear, or animal hair may be used to partially obscure the features and heighten the comic effect. Because symmetry, proportion, and subtle transition between forms are so basic to the Mende ideal, Gongoli is a caricature. He is also a satirist and a prankster as he dances during celebrations or visits the houses of the recently bereaved to cheer them. Gongoli is one of the few men's masks allowed to speak; he takes advantage of his prerogative, often insulting the spectators. As a mimic he keeps the crowd amused, while the real spirits of the secret societies retire to rest. He staggers around like a drunk and eventually sinks to the ground in a stupor.

Folk tales characterize him as being a trickster, fond of winning competitions with Gonde[1] by his wit. Whenever the two dance together Gongoli is the best and the liveliest. Once they were supposed to have a race around the village. Gonde ran as fast as she could around the whole perimeter. Gongoli stood mocking the crowd as they urged him to catch up. Finally, he ambled leisurely around one hut, returned to the finish point, and announced he had won. In answer to the protests of the townspeople he replied, "What is a village but a home?"

The humorous masks play an important part in serious ceremonies by offering comic relief. At first it would seem their sole function is entertainment; however, Gongoli is commonly fed by placing chewed kolanuts in the mouth, an action usually reserved for sacrificial offering to a spirit. This act could be the carry-over of an obsolete ritual, or a retention of vestigial spiritual force.

Gongoli amuses by being ridiculous and insulting; the Tondo couple entertains by combining absurdity with eroticism. Both masks are danced by men. The "male" wears a wooden helmet painted in red and pink stripes with two notches for eyes and a raffia tuft on top. His face and body are covered with a garment of red and pink print; the sleeves cover the hands, and the legs flare out over the feet. Under his costume he carries a ball-like object which he manipulates in front of his groin during the dance. The "female" headpiece is red and pink striped metal which flares out from the head to a flat top. A long beak-like projection extends down in front of her heavily padded breasts. Accompanied by a drummer playing on a flat, square instrument painted to match the Tondo headpieces, the two execute a series of obviously erotic gyrations and undulations in their dance which evokes bursts of laughter.

Like Gongoli, they appear to be strictly entertainers and have no present affiliation with a particular society or spirit. Yet the similarity of their dance to a Njayei ceremony suggests the performance may originally have been intended to elicit assistance through sympathy as the human activity was equated with the spiritual bestowal of fertility on land and people.

[1]It is sometimes told as being Bundu, but it would be out of character for the Bundu spirit to engage in such frivolity.

GONGOLI, NAFOLI, Kpetema,
Begba Chiefdom, Bo District

64. GONGOLI MASK WITH COWRIE SHELLS AND
ANIMAL HAIR, 27
Lent Anonymously

57. GONGOLI MASK WITH RAFFIA, 24¾
Collected at Yoni, Sitia Chiefdom, Sherbro
Island, Bonthe District, 1936–37
Collection of the University Museum, Uni-
versity of Pennsylvania, Philadelphia

56. GONGOLI MASK, 20
Collected near Pujehun
Collection of Michael Heidi, Seattle

61. GONGOLI MASK WITH MONKEY FUR, 21½
Collection of the Museum of African Art,
Washington, D.C.
Gift of Mr. and Mrs. Leonard Whitehouse

69. NOMOLI FIGURE, 5½
     Soapstone
     Sherbro
     Collection of The Museum of Primitive
     Art, New York

Nomoli Figures

Nomoli figures of soapstone or other soft stone, probably carved by the Sherbro or Bulom as early as the 15th century, have frequently been unearthed by the Mende in the process of cultivating their rice fields.[1] Their bulging forms are symbolic of fertility, relating to the swelling of a germinated seed. Most are male figures and are found buried in the earth, Ngewo's wife, giving them a phallic significance, thus associating them with an older ancestor/fertility cult which uses the natural phallic form of the white ant's nest. These nests are sometimes hollowed out and Nomoli placed in them, combining the two traditions. If a farmer does not find a Nomoli in his field, he may erect a shrine with three sticks placed in the ground, an invitation for the ants to form their nests around the sticks. In this case the male symbolism is found in the phallic form and the male number.

Nomoli are ancestors who bring the blessings of fertility, not immediate ancestors, but rather the spirits of the first farmers. The realm of the deceased spirits is below the ground; thus, it is only natural that the Nomoli are found in the ground. The relationship between farmer and Nomoli is best expressed by the words spoken while the figure is ceremonially flogged. "I have boiled rice today and have given you your portion; now go and bring plenty for me."[2] Nomoli is responsible for the flourishing of the rice crop in the field where his shrine is located. The figure is either punished or rewarded according to the results of the harvest. The figures are not only used to petition the ancestors for a good crop and to thank or complain to them about the harvest, but also to protect the farmer and his family.

The dispersion of these figures throughout a large area of Sierra Leone and the fact that none of them have been found above ground indicates their use in some type of burial ceremony. Among the Kissi, who live to the east of the Mende, a similar figure is also associated with the ancestral cult. The person who discovers the figure in the ground uses it as a medium of contact with one of his immediate ancestors. Upon his death the figure is buried with him. A similar situation may have existed among the Sherbro who sometimes use unsculpted stone to contact their ancestors.

Since the immediate ancestors are the most important link between man and God, a figure which housed the ancestor spirit loses its importance upon the death of its immediate descendant. In the case of wood sculpture, the figure soon deteriorates; however, the soapstone figure does not. Therefore, the figure may have been buried with its descendants in a practice similar to that of the Kissi.

While symmetry and balance appear to be an important aesthetic criteria for the Nomoli figure, the bold forms and bulging treatment of the body present a contrast to the delicacy of most Mende sculpture.

[1]This attribution is supported by the stylistic similarity between the Nomoli and the figures on the ivory spoons and salt cellars created by the Sherbro artists for the Portuguese during the fifteenth and sixteenth centuries.

[2]Stanley Brown, "The Nomoli of Mende Country," *Africa* 18, no. 1 (January 1948), p. 19.

71. SPOON, 8⅞
     Ivory
     Sherbro-Portuguese
     Collection of The Museum of Primitive
     Art, New York
72. SPOON, 6⅜
     Ivory
     Sherbro-Portuguese
     Collection of the Museum of African Art,
     Washington, D.C.
     Gift of Mrs. Robert Woods Bliss Estate

Ancestor Figures

The seated female figure is used in ceremonies by the Mende to petition the ancestors for help. The Mende, like other African peoples have created several means of communication with their ancestors.

The figure is seated on a stool, but often the figure and the stool become such an integral form that the front legs of the stool are omitted and the seat is supported by the woman's legs. Often the breasts are enlarged to emphasize the fertility and motherly aspects of this spiritual contact. The figures are spoken of as wise women and are consulted in much the same manner as an elderly woman of the village is asked for advice.

The seated position and the interplay of voids and solids around the stool and in front of the figure create a very different sculptural expression from the more compact form of other Mende figures. This openness draws the observer into the figure, and this receptiveness establishes and characterizes the spiritual relationship.

73. SEATED ANCESTOR FIGURE, 22½
Pujehun District
Collection of Dr. and Mrs. Bernard Berk,
Lutherville, Md.

Twin Figures

Unlike other Mende sculpture, twin figures are carved with moveable arms which make them easy to dress. Because twins are thought to be possessed of special powers either to bring death to parents and friends or to promote fertility and protect pregnant women, their birth is met with mixed emotions, and special procedures are followed. The first born is always called Sao or Salo and the second Jina. Should one die, a figure is carved to house its spirit; the sculpture is given the same care as the survivor and dressed in the same clothes lest it feel neglected and harm the living twin.

74. TWIN FIGURE, 24
Collection of Mrs. Sonja Holsey, Washington, D.C.

Wunde Fetish

The Wunde, men's society found mainly among the Kpa-Mende where it is considered more powerful than Poro, keeps a fetish which embodies a protective spirit. A fetish, by definition, gains its life force through the materials used in its creation. In the case of the Wunde fetish this power is transmitted by clay and cowrie shells—both symbols of fertility. Similar to the Nomoli soapstone in their robust forms, the figures also communicate the concept of fertility to the spirits.

Little of the symbolism and functions of these figures is divulged to non-initiates of the society. It is known, however, that the Wunde performs fertility ceremonies as well as birth and marriage rituals. Its main public function is a dance in which a fire, symbolizing life, is protected by the inner circle of members while an outer circle tries to extinguish it. Three members dressed as women intermingle as peacemakers. The ceremony is a manifestation of the Wunde's control of life force; the fetish figure may be a sculptural analogy to it.

75. WUNDE FETISH WITH COWRIE SHELLS, 29
Collection of Dr. and Mrs. Bernard Berk,
Lutherville, Md.

Hammock Bars

Even the bar, used to hold each end of the hammock open, takes on an intricate sculptural form in the hands of a master carver. Two different approaches are demonstrated by the pieces in this exhibition. One artist conceived of the bars as extensions of the hammock and carved the ends as complex knots. The texture of the twine used in the hammock is simulated in these knots and contrasted with the smooth treatment of the centers.

The other more closely resembles authority staffs or heddle pulleys in which the typical Mende head emerges from the ends of the sculpture. The linear treatment of the hairstyle is repeated in the neck ridges. The eyes and mouth repeat the same outline, a characteristic which can be noted in many Bundu masks. The ridges, which hold the hammock ropes, are incised to relate to the design of the hair and neck. The center bulges add a feeling of strength to the object.

These are beautiful examples of sculpture, which are made with no symbolic importance. They demonstrate how the artist can invent or use traditional forms for the decoration of utilitarian objects.

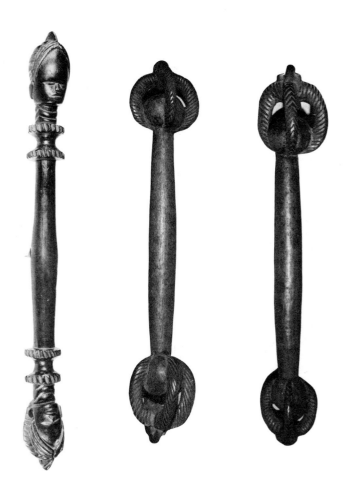

76. HAMMOCK BAR WITH HEADS, 14⅛
    Collection of the UCLA Museum of Cultural History Gift of Mr. and Mrs. Ralph Altman
77. HAMMOCK BARS WITH CARVED ROPE LOOPS (PAIR), 13½
    Collected at Mobambi, Sitia Chiefdom, Sherbro Island, Bonthe District, 1936–37
    Collection of the University Museum, University of Pennsylvania, Philadelphia

Authority Staffs

The decoration of authority staffs ranges from abstract geometric designs to carvings of humans and animals. Usually associated with the chief's prestige, they are carried on certain occasions to show his position in the community. Often there is a fertility symbol on the staff relating the chief's position as intermediary between the people and the ancestors in the religious structure. Because of his close relationship with the spirits, the chief is responsible for the material and spiritual well-being of the community.

The similarity between the decorations on some authority staffs and the figure sculpture used by the women's societies suggests that they may be used by the leaders of these societies. When the Bundu spirit performs a dance in public, she often carries an uncarved stick. It is possible that these authority staffs, decorated with female figures, are used in their secret rituals.

The artist creates a head or figure from the columnar handle. The balance and delicacy is consistent with the larger sculpture.

78. AUTHORITY STAFF WITH FEMALE FIGURE, 33
Collected near Bo
Collection of Michael Heide, Seattle

82. AUTHORITY STAFF WITH FEMALE FIGURE, 36¼
Collection of The Museum of Primitive Art, New York

79. AUTHORITY STAFF WITH FEMALE FIGURE, 40
Carved in Timdel Chiefdom, Moyamba District, Collected 1936–37
Collection of the University Museum, University of Pennsylvania, Philadelphia
81. AUTHORITY STAFF WITH WOMAN ON STOOL, 37¼
Collected at Shenge, Kagboro Chiefdom, Moyamba District, 1937
Collection of the University Museum, University of Pennsylvania, Philadelphia

Heddle Pulleys

The heddle, or weaving pulley, on the upper part of looms used to produce long narrow pieces of "country cloth" are sometimes decorated with sculptures resembling Bundu masks and Sande medicine heads.

Since the Mende call upon ancestors and other spirits for help and protection whenever they undertake a project, the sculpture may be an invitation for the spirit to enter the loom. The majority of Mende looms, however, have plain pulleys; only the prosperous can afford the ostentation of sculpture.

84. HEDDLE PULLEY, 8¾
    Collected at Tisana, Dema Chiefdom, Sherbro Island, Bonthe District, 1936–37
    Collection of the University Museum, University of Pennsylvania, Philadelphia
85. HEDDLE PULLEY, 7¾
    Collection of Mr. and Mrs. Harold Rome, New York
86. TEI GAME BOARD, 25
    Collection of Robert and Nancy Nooter, Washington, D.C.

Tei Game Board

The game board, which is found throughout Africa as well as in other parts of the world, is known by many names. Among the Mende, it derives its name from the tei seeds that are moved in the playing of the game.

Because it is a very popular game, the variation in the sculptural quality of the board is great, the only constant being the use of twelve depressions. The game board can be formed from a rectangular piece of wood with no other ornamentation, or it can become an intricate piece of sculpture.

The example in the exhibition is carved with intertwining forms which create both a feeling of openness and solidity. The intricacy of design attests to the artist's ability to translate his visual image into sculptural form.

Alldridge, T. J. "Wanderings in the Hinterland of Sierra Leone." *The Geographical Journal,* 4, no. 2 (August 1894) pp. 123–140.
Earliest description of the Mende Bundu masks and dancers.
————. *The Sherbro and Its Hinterland.* New York, 1910.
The appearance and function of the Bundu spirit as well as the Yassi ceremonies are vividly discussed.
————. *A Transformed Colony—Sierra Leone.* London, 1910.
Excellent account of Sande dismissal ceremony and customs which accompany it.
Brown, Stanley. "The Nomoli of Mende Country." *Africa,* 18, No. 1 (January 1948).
Discusses the position of the Nomoli in the Mende culture and its association with spirits. Good description of the forms of these figures.
Gervis, Pearce. *Sierra Leone Story.* London, 1952.
Includes a valuable account by a woman physician of the Sande initiation rite
Hall, H. U. *The Sherbro of Sierra Leone.* Philadelphia, 1938.
Describes the Yassi, Sande, Poro, and Humoi which are common to the Mende and Sherbro.
Little, Kenneth L. "The Role of the Secret Society in Cultural Specialization." *American Anthropologist,* n.s. 51, no. 2 (1949) pp. 199–212.
This article is a valuable study of many of the Mende organizations. Concentrating on the Poro educational and political functions and the Yassi and Humoi medical and sexual control functions.
————. *The Mende of Sierra Leone.* London, 1951.
Particularly valuable are the discussions of the Poro, Sande, Njayei, and Humoi.
———— "The Mende of Sierra Leone." *African Worlds.* Edited by Daryll Forde, London, 1954.
A brief but excellent study similar to his previously cited publication.
McCulloch, Merran. *Peoples of Sierra Leone.* London, 1950.
Contains valuable ethnographic information on the Mende and other Sierra Leone cultures.
Migoed, F.W.H. *A View of Sierra Leone.* London, 1926.
Discusses the variations in the Sande and Poro among the Mende and their neighboring cultures.
Newland, H. Osman. *Sierra Leone: Its People, Products, Secret Societies.* London, 1916.
Provides some excellent early information on the Mende Bundu, Poro, and Yassi, concentrating on initiation rites.
Sawyerr, Harry. *God: Ancestor or Creator?* London, 1970.
Includes an interesting study of Mende religion.

The Mende, numbering about 700,000 and the largest ethnic group in Sierra Leone, live in the southern part of the country but are linguistically related to the Mande-speaking peoples of Guinea and Mali. Besides the three main divisions of Kpa-, Ko-, and Sewa Mende, there are many groups which resulted from the acculturation of neighboring peoples, the Sherbro and Vai. They are ruled by a hierarchy of chiefs having a paramount chief as head of each district. Their economy is based on rice farming.

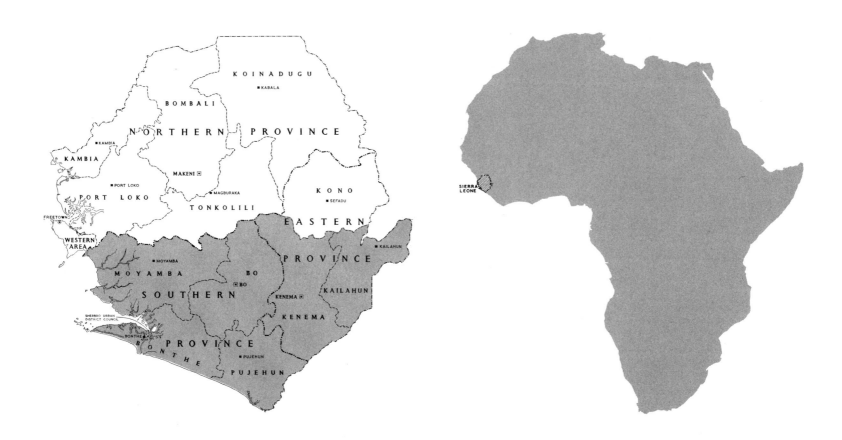

KOINADUGU

KABALA

BOMBALI

NORTHERN PROVINCE

KAMBIA

KAMBIA

MAKENI

PORT LOKO

PORT LOKO

KONO

MAGBURAKA

SEFADU

FREETOWN

TONKOLILI

EASTERN

WESTERN
AREA

MOYAMBA

PROVINCE

KAILAHUN

MOYAMBA

BO

SOUTHERN

BO

KAILAHUN

KENEMA

SHERBRO URBAN
DISTRICT COUNCIL

KENEMA

PROVINCE

BONTHE

BONTHE

PUJEHUN

PUJEHUN

PUJEHUN

SIERRA
LEONE

Catalog of the Exhibition

All objects are of wood unless otherwise noted. Measurements in inches are given for greatest dimension.

1. BUNDU MASK WITH RAFFIA, 15
   Carved 1896, Sembehun, Moyamba District
   Collection of Dr. Joseph Seipp, Baltimore
2. BUNDU MASK, 18¾
   Carved 1906, Mano Chiefdom, Moyamba District
   Collection of Dr. Joseph Seipp, Baltimore
3. BUNDU MASK, 15
   Carved 1918, Mano Chiefdom, Moyamba District
   Collection of Dr. Joseph Seipp, Baltimore
4. BUNDU MASK, 15
   Carved 1918, Mano Chiefdom, Moyamba District
   Collection of Martin Fredmann, Baltimore
5. BUNDU MASK WITH SILVER, 15
   Collection of Dr. and Mrs. Bernard Berk, Lutherville, Md.
6. BUNDU MASK, 16½
   Vai-Mende
   Collection of the UCLA Museum of Cultural History, Gift of the Wellcome Trust
7. BUNDU MASK, 14
   Collection of Mrs. Judith Kahan, New York
8. BUNDU MASK, 15½
   Collection of the New Orleans Museum of Art
   Gift of Mr. and Mrs. Walter Davis, Jr.
9. BUNDU MASK, 18⅛
   Collection of The Brooklyn Museum, Brooklyn, N.Y.
10. BUNDU MASK, 13¾
    Vai-Mende
    Collection of The Museum of Primitive Art, New York

11. BUNDU MASK, 25
    Mother and Child
    Kpa-Mende
    Collection of The Museum of Primitive Art, New York
12. BUNDU MASK, 15
    Boyadu, Kenema District
    Lent Anonymously
13. BUNDU MASK, 16
    Kowama, Moyamba District
    Lent Anonymously
14. BUNDU MASK, 11½
    Mamba, Bonthe District
    Collection of the Museum of African Art, Washington, D.C.
    Gift of Mr. Frederick Richman
15. BUNDU MASK, 16
    Collection of Robert and Nancy Nooter, Washington, D.C.
16. BUNDU MASK, 17½
    Carved by Moisi, Nganyahun, Moyamba District
    Lent Anonymously
17. BUNDU MASK, 16
    Carved by Moisi
    Collection of the Art Gallery, University of Maryland, College Park
18. BUNDU MASK WITH METAL, 14
    Collection of Joseph J. Barghahn
19. BUNDU MASK, 15
    Collection of Joseph J. Barghahn
20. BUNDU MASK, 18
    Collection of Joseph J. Barghahn
21. BUNDU FIGURE MASK, 26
    Collection of Joseph J. Barghahn
22. BUNDU MASK, 15
    Vai-Mende
    Collection of Joseph J. Barghahn
23. GONDE MASK WITH COSTUME, 15
    Collected at Bembe, Sitia Chiefdom
    Sherbro Island, Bonthe District, 1936–37
    Collection of the University Museum, University of Pennsylvania, Philadelphia

24. GONDE HELMET WITH SMALL HEAD, 14
    Collection of Dr. and Mrs. Bernard Berk, Lutherville, Md.
25. SANDE (GONDE HELMET?) FIGURE, 16
    Collection of Barbara J. Jacoby, Los Angeles
26. SANDE MEDICINE HEAD, 9
    Collected at Mokele, Kagboro Chiefdom
    Sherbro Island, Bonthe District, 1936–37
    Collection of the University Museum, University of Pennsylvania, Philadelphia
27. SANDE MEDICINE FIGURE, 23½
    Collection of the Museum of African Art, Washington, D.C.
    Gift of Robert and Nancy Nooter
28. SANDE MEDICINE HEAD, 14
    Carved by Moisi, Nganyahun, Moyamba District
    Lent Anonymously
29. SANDE MEDICINE HEAD, 11⅝
    Collection of the UCLA Museum of Cultural History
    Gift of the Wellcome Trust
30. MUSICAL STAFF WITH TWO HEADS, 18¼
    Carved at Sembehu, Sitia Chiefdom, Sherbro Island, Bonthe District
    Collected 1936–37
    Collection of the University Museum, University of Pennsylvania, Philadelphia
31. MUSICAL STAFF WITH WOMAN'S COIFFURE, 19
    Collected from Chief of Tome
    Sherbro Island, Bonthe District, 1936–37
    Collection of the University Museum, University of Pennsylvania, Philadelphia
32. GOBOI
    Raffia, leather, cloth and wood
    Collected from Bumpe Chiefdom, Bo District, 1929
    Collection of the University Museum, University of Pennsylvania, Philadelphia

33. NAFOLI HEADPIECE, 18
Leather, mirrors, and fur
Vai-Mende
Collection of The American Museum of
Natural History, New York

34. NJAYEI MASK WITH RAFFIA, 21
Lent Anonymously

35. MEDICINE FIGURE, 29
Collection of Michael Heide, Seattle

36. MEDICINE FIGURE, 29
Collection of Mr. and Mrs. Harold Rome,
New York

37. MEDICINE FIGURE, 16¼
Collection of The Museum of Primitive
Art, New York

38. MEDICINE FIGURE, 27
Collection of The American Museum of
Natural History, New York

39. MEDICINE FIGURE, 20½
Collection of The American Museum of
Natural History, New York

40. MEDICINE FIGURE, 36½
Vai-Mende
Collection of The American Museum of
Natural History, New York

41. MEDICINE FIGURE, 27¾
Collection of Barbara J. Jacoby, Los Angeles

42. MEDICINE FIGURE, 20
Collection of the Museum of African Art,
Washington, D.C.
Gift of Lawrence Gussman

43. MEDICINE FIGURE WITH BEADS, 10
Collection of Mr. and Mrs. James M.
Silberman, Arlington, Va.

44. MEDICINE FIGURE, 32
Carved by Amadu Kamara, Regent, Western Area
Collection of the Art Gallery, University
of Maryland, College Park.

45. MEDICINE FIGURE, 16½
Collection of the Baltimore Museum of Art
Wurtzburger Collection

46. YASSI MEDICINE FIGURE IN BOWL, WITH
ALUMINUM, 17¾
Collected at Kawno, Sitia Chiefdom, Sherbro Island, Bonthe District, 1936–37
Collection of the University Museum, University of Pennsylvania, Philadelphia

47. MEDICINE FIGURE, 23½
Collected at Bembe, Sitia Chiefdom, Sherbro Island, Bonthe District, 1936–37
Collection of the University Museum, University of Pennsylvania, Philadelphia

48. MEDICINE FIGURE, 22¾
Collected at Yoni, Sitia Chiefdom, Sherbro Island, Bonthe District, 1936–37
Collection of the University Museum, University of Pennsylvania, Philadelphia

49. MEDICINE FIGURE, 12
Collection of Joseph J. Barghahn

50. MEDICINE FIGURE. 12¾
Collection of Joseph J. Barghahn

51. MEDICINE FIGURE, 20½
Collection of Joseph J. Barghahn

52. MEDICINE FIGURE WITH BEADS, 20¾
Collection of Joseph J. Barghahn

53. MEDICINE FIGURE WITH BEADS, 22
Collection of Joseph J. Barghahn

54. CLAY MORTAR, 11
Collection of the UCLA Museum of Cultural History, Gift of the Wellcome Trust

55. CLAY MORTAR, 12½
Collection of the UCLA Museum of Cultural History, Gift of the Wellcome Trust

56. GONGOLI MASK, 20
Collected near Pujehun
Collection of Michael Heidi, Seattle

57. GONGOLI MASK WITH RAFFIA, 24¾
Collected at Yoni, Sitia Chiefdom, Sherbro Island, Bonthe District, 1936–37
Collection of the University Museum, University of Pennsylvania, Philadelphia

58. GONGOLI MASK, 14¼
Collected at Mokebe, Kagboro Chiefdom, Moyamba District, 1936–37
Collection of the University Museum, University of Pennsylvania, Philadelphia

59. GONGOLI MASK, 34¾
Collection of The Brooklyn Museum, Brooklyn, N.Y.

60. GONGOLI MASK, 19
Collection of the American Museum of Natural History, New York

61. GONGOLI MASK WITH MONKEY FUR, 21½
Collection of the Museum of African Art, Washington, D.C.
Gift of Mr. and Mrs. Leonard Whitehouse

62. GONGOLI MASK, 24
Collection of the Museum of African Art, Washington, D.C.
Gift of Robert and Nancy Nooter

63. GONGOLI MASK, 22½
Collection of the Museum of African Art, Washington, D.C.
Gift of Eliot Elisofon

64. GONGOLI MASK WITH COWRIE SHELLS AND
ANIMAL HAIR, 27
Lent Anonymously

65. GONGOLI MASK, 25
Lent Anonymously

66. GONGOLI MASK, 17½
Carved by Amadu Kamara, Regent, Western Area
Collection of the Art Gallery, University of Maryland, College Park.

67. GONGOLI MASK, 12½
Carved by Amadu Kamara, Regent, Western Area
Collection of the Art Gallery, University of Maryland, College Park.

68. GONGOLI MASK, 12½
Carved by Amadu Kamara, Regent, Western Area
Collection of the Art Gallery, University of Maryland, College Park.

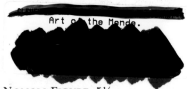

Art of the Mende.

69. NOMOLI FIGURE, 5½
Soapstone
Sherbro
Collection of The Museum of Primitive
Art, New York

70. NOMOLI FIGURE, 5½
Soapstone
Sherbro
Collection of Robert and Nancy Nooter,
Washington, D.C.

71. SPOON, 8⅞
Ivory
Sherbro-Portuguese
Collection of The Museum of Primitive
Art, New York

72. SPOON, 6⅜
Ivory
Sherbro-Portuguese
Collection of the Museum of African Art,
Washington, D.C.
Gift of Mrs. Robert Woods Bliss Estate

73. SEATED ANCESTOR FIGURE, 22½
Pujehun District
Collection of Dr. and Mrs. Bernard Berk,
Lutherville, Md.

74. TWIN FIGURE, 24
Collection of Mrs. Sonja Holsey, Washington, D.C.

75. WUNDE FETISH WITH COWRIE SHELLS, 29
Collection of Dr. and Mrs. Bernard Berk,
Lutherville, Md.

76. HAMMOCK BAR WITH HEADS, 14⅛
Collection of the UCLA Museum of Cul-
tural History Gift of Mr. and Mrs. Ralph
Altman

77. HAMMOCK BARS WITH CARVED ROPE
LOOPS (PAIR), 13½
Collected at Mobambi, Sitia Chiefdom,
Sherbro Island, Bonthe District, 1936–37
Collection of the University Museum, Uni-
versity of Pennsylvania, Philadelphia

78. AUTHORITY STAFF WITH FEMALE FIGURE,
33
Collected near Bo
Collection of Michael Heide, Seattle

79. AUTHORITY STAFF WITH FEMALE FIGURE,
40
Carved in Timdel Chiefdom, Moyamba
District, Collected 1936–37
Collection of the University Museum, Uni-
versity of Pennsylvania, Philadelphia

81. AUTHORITY STAFF WITH MONKEY, 50½
Collected at Yoni, Sitia Chiefdom, Sherbro Island, Bonthe District, 1936–37
Collection of the University Museum, University of Pennsylvania, Philadelphia

81. AUTHORITY STAFF WITH WOMAN ON
STOOL, 37¼
Collected at Shenge, Kagboro Chiefdom,
Moyamba District, 1937
Collection of the University Museum, Uni-
versity of Pennsylvania, Philadelphia

82. AUTHORITY STAFF WITH FEMALE FIGURE,
36¼
Collection of The Museum of Primitive
Art, New York

83. AUTHORITY STAFF WITH FEMALE HEAD,
31½
Collection of the Museum of African Art,
Washington, D.C.
Gift of James W. Moseley

84. HEDDLE PULLEY, 8¾
Collected at Tisana, Dema Chiefdom,
Sherbro Island, Bonthe District, 1936–37
Collection of the University Museum, Uni-
versity of Pennsylvania, Philadelphia

85. HEDDLE PULLEY, 7¾
Collection of Mr. and Mrs. Harold Rome,
New York

86. TEI GAME BOARD, 25
Collection of Robert and Nancy Nooter,
Washington, D.C.